46 Cavity Preventing Meal Recipes:

Strengthen Your Teeth and Your Oral Health by Eating Nutrient Packed Foods

By

Joe Correa CSN

COPYRIGHT

© 2016 Live Stronger Faster Inc.

All rights reserved

Reproduction or translation of any part of this work beyond that permitted by section 107 or 108 of the 1976 United States Copyright Act without the permission of the copyright owner is unlawful.

This publication is designed to provide accurate and authoritative information in regard to the subject matter covered. It is sold with the understanding that neither the author nor the publisher is engaged in rendering medical advice. If medical advice or assistance is needed, consult with a doctor. This book is considered a guide and should not be used in any way detrimental to your health. Consult with a physician before starting this nutritional plan to make sure it's right for you.

ACKNOWLEDGEMENTS

This book is dedicated to my friends and family that have had mild or serious illnesses so that you may find a solution and make the necessary changes in your life.

46 Cavity Preventing Meal Recipes:

Strengthen Your Teeth and Your Oral Health by Eating Nutrient Packed Foods

By

Joe Correa CSN

CONTENTS

Copyright

Acknowledgements

About The Author

Introduction

46 Cavity Preventing Meal Recipes: Strengthen Your Teeth and Your Oral Health by Eating Nutrient Packed Foods

Additional Titles from This Author

ABOUT THE AUTHOR

After years of Research, I honestly believe in the positive effects that proper nutrition can have over the body and mind. My knowledge and experience has helped me live healthier throughout the years and which I have shared with family and friends. The more you know about eating and drinking healthier, the sooner you will want to change your life and eating habits.

Nutrition is a key part in the process of being healthy and living longer so get started today. The first step is the most important and the most significant.

INTRODUCTION

We brush twice a day, we floss daily, we rinse our mouth with mouthwash. But what about food? There is a big chance that the secret to healthy teeth can be found in the refrigerator!

In order to prevent cavities and to maintain a beautiful smile, you need to take into consideration your diet, what you eat, and how often do you eat. You will be surprised to see that the changes will start right after you eat certain foods!

In daily life, our teeth have a lot of enemies such as sticky snacks, sugary sodas, treats and much more. Lucky for us, there are foods that prevent tooth decay.

It may be a real challenge to maintain a cavity free mouth. Some studies show that over 92% of adults between 20 and 64 have had cavities in their permanent teeth.

Include these recipes in your daily diet and you should see major changes happening in no time!

46 CAVITY PREVENTING MEAL RECIPES: STRENGTHEN YOUR TEETH AND YOUR ORAL HEALTH BY EATING NUTRIENT PACKED FOODS

1. **Grande Pomegranate Salad**
   - Description:
     Pomegranate is a good source of fibre. It also contains vitamins A, C and E, iron and other antioxidants.
   - Ingredients:
     - 2 pomegranates, peeled and seeds separated
     - 2 cans mandarin orange segments
     - 1 red onion, chopped
     - 1 jalapeno pepper, minced
     - 1 tablespoon minced pickled jalapeno pepper
     - 1 bunch cilantro, minced
     - 1 lime, juiced
   - How to prepare:

- ➢ Mix pomegranate seeds, mandarin oranges, onion, fresh jalapeno, pickled jalapeno, cilantro, lime juice, and cumin together in a bowl.
- ➢ Cover bowl and refrigerate for several hours or overnight to let flavors blend.
- Nutritional facts:
  Calories: 57kcal, Fat: 0.2g, Carbs: 14g, Protein: 1.1g, Sodium: 26mg

2. Mr. Cranberry's Salad

- Description:

  Cranberries are a very good source of vitamin C, dietary fiber, and manganese, as well as a good source of vitamin E, vitamin K, copper and pantothenic acid.

- Ingredients:
  - 1 1/2 cups chopped cranberries
  - 1 cup chopped red apple
  - 1 cup chopped celery
  - 1 cup seedless green grapes
  - 1/3 cup raisins
  - 1/4 cup chopped walnuts
  - 1/4 teaspoon ground cinnamon
  - 1 (8 ounce) low-fat yogurt

- How to prepare:
  - In a medium bowl, combine cranberries, apple, celery, grapes, raisins, walnuts, sugar, cinnamon, and yogurt. Toss to coat. Cover, and chill 2 hours. Stir just before serving.

- Nutritional facts:

Calories: 75kcal, Fat: 2g, Carbs: 1.7g, Protein: 22g, Sodium: 26mg

3. Mrs. Mozaic Salsa

- Description:

  Oranges are an excellent source of vitamin C. They are also a very good source of dietary fiber. In addition, oranges are a good source of B vitamins including vitamin B1, pantothenic acid and folate as well as vitamin A, calcium, copper and potassium

- Ingredients:
  - 2 large oranges, peeled and cut into chunks
  - 1 tomato, seeded and diced
  - 1/2 cup minced red onion
  - 1 tablespoon apple juice
  - 1 teaspoon grated orange zest
  - 1 teaspoon minced garlic
  - 1/4 jalapeno pepper, minced
  - 1 tablespoon chopped fresh cilantro

- How to prepare:
  - Combine oranges, tomato, onion, apple juice, orange zest, garlic, and jalapeno pepper in a large bowl; toss to combine. Cover and

refrigerate until chilled, about 30 minutes.

Stir in cilantro before serving.

- Nutritional facts:

Calories: 41kcal, Fat: 0.1g, Carbs: 10g, Protein: 1g, Sodium: 2mg

4. Pear Benefactor

- Description:

  Only one pear contains up to 11 percent of our daily recommended intake of vitamin C and 10% of our daily recommended intake of copper. Pears are also said to have more nutrients per calorie than calorie per nutrient.

- Ingredients:
  - 1 ripe pear - peeled, cored, and chopped
  - 1/2 cup white wine
  - 1 clove garlic, chopped
  - 1/4 cup white balsamic vinegar
  - 1 teaspoon ground black pepper
  - 1/4 teaspoon sea salt
  - 1/2 cup olive oil

- How to prepare:
  - Blend the pear, white wine, garlic, white balsamic vinegar, black pepper, and sea salt in a blender until well combined; drizzle the olive oil into the mixture in a thin, steady stream while continuing to blend. Blend a

few seconds longer until the salad dressing is thick and creamy.

- Nutritional facts:

  Calories : 101kcal, Fat : 9g, Carbs : 3.6g, Protein : 0.1g, Sodium : 60mg

5. Radishlicious

- **Description**

   Radishes contain Vitamin C and antioxidants, which makes them quite effective in preventing cavities. Regular inclusion of radishes in your diet results in healthy teeth and gums.

- **Ingredients:**

   - 20 radishes
   - 2 tablespoon water
   - 1 tablespoon olive oil
   - salt and pepper to taste

- **How to prepare:**

   - Trim the ends off of the radishes and peel a band of radish-skin from around the middle of the radish.
   - Steam the radishes in a covered microwave safe container for 8 minutes, or until fork tender, serve immediately.

- Nutritional facts:

  Calories:109 Fat:11.6g, Carbs:1.5g, Protein:0.4g, Sodium : 106mg

6. Rhubarb Guard

- Description:

  Rhubarb is full of minerals, vitamins, organic compounds, and other nutrients that make it ideal for keeping cavities away and our bodies healthy.

- Ingredients:
  - 1/2 cup water
  - 3 cups thinly sliced rhubarb
  - 15 seedless grapes
  - 1/2 orange, sectioned
  - 10 fresh strawberries
  - 1 apple, cored and diced
  - 1 peach, sliced
  - 1 plum, sliced

- How to prepare:
  - Bring water to boil in a medium saucepan over medium heat. Stir in the rhubarb, turn heat to low, cover, and simmer until rhubarb is soft, 10 to 15 minutes. Mash and chill in the refrigerator, about one hour.

- Stir gently, but thoroughly to coat. Refrigerate for at least two hours to allow the flavors to blend.
- Nutritional facts:

  Calories : 236kcal, Fat : 0.9g, Carbs : 59g, Protein : 1.9g, Sodium : 6mg

7. Fair Raspberry

- Description:

   Red Raspberries contain strong antioxidants such as Vitamin C, quercetin and gallic acid. Research has shown that maintaining a good balance of oxidants and antioxidants is important for oral health, as well as systemic health.

- Ingredients:
  - 1 pound mixed salad greens
  - 1 pint fresh raspberries
  - 4 ounces slivered almonds
  - 1 cup raspberry vinaigrette

- How to prepare:
  - Toss salad greens, raspberries, and almonds together in a large bowl. Drizzle with raspberry vinaigrette to serve.

- Nutritional facts:

   Calories : 182kcal, Fat : 7g, Carbs : 25g, Protein : 4.7g, Sodium : 350mg

8. **Cavity Fighter**
   - Description:

     This smoothie contains everything you need to stay strong in front of decay. Include this in your daily diet and see results in no time!
   - Ingredients:
     - 1 cup milk 1 1/2 bananas
   - How to prepare:
     - Blend milk and bananas in a blender or food processor until smooth.
   - Nutritional facts:

     Calories : 280kcal, Fat : 5.4g, Carbs : 56g, Protein : 10g, Sodium : 102mg

9. Kung Fu Kefir

- Description:

    Kefir is a fermented milk product (cow, goat or sheep milk) that tastes like a drinkable yogurt. Kefir contains high levels of vitamin B12, calcium, magnesium, vitamin K2, biotin, folate, enzymes and probiotics.

- Ingredients:
    - 4 cups milk
    - 1/2 cup plain kefir
- How to prepare:
    - Preheat a yogurt maker or slow cooker on Low.
    - Whisk milk in a saucepan over medium heat until almost boiling, about 4 minutes.
    - Gently stir kefir into milk mixture until just blended. Pour mixture into yogurt containers or slow cooker.
    -
    - Cook on Low until the desired level of tartness and yogurt consistency is reached, 4

to 10 hours. Chill yogurt in the refrigerator, at least 2 hours.

- Nutritional facts:

 Calories : 84kcal, Fat : 2.9g, Carbs : 8.4g, Protein : 5.7g, Sodium : 77mg

10. Cloud Nine

- Description:

  Bananas are excellent cavity protectors for your teeth. They provide several necessary nutrients to benefit digestion, heart health and weight loss. This recipe is fast and easy.

- Ingredients:
  - 1 banana
  - 1/2 cup yogurt
  - 1/4 cup pineapple juice
  - 1 cup strawberries
  - 1 teaspoon orange juice
  - 1 teaspoon milk

- How to prepare:
  - Blend the banana, yogurt, sugar, pineapple juice, strawberries, orange juice, and milk in a blender until smooth.

- Nutritional facts:

  Calories : 147kcal, Fat : 1.4g, Carbs : 31.3g, Protein : 4.6g, Sodium : 46mg

11. Lemon Flavour Salmon

- Description:

    Long known to be beneficial for general bone health, vitamin D boosts your calcium metabolism and induces cathelicidin, which is an antimicrobial peptide that attacks the bacteria known to cause dental cavities. Lucky for us, Vitamin D can be found in salmon

- Ingredients:
    - 1 (16 ounce) red salmon, drained and flaked
    - 1 lemon, juiced
    - 1 apple, cored and minced
    - 1 1/2 stalks celery, chopped fine
    - 1/4 teaspoon crushed red pepper flakes

- How to prepare:
    - Combine red salmon and lemon juice in a glass bowl; mix well.
    - Stir in apple, celery and crushed red pepper flakes; mix thoroughly.

- Nutritional facts:

    Calories: 368kcal, Fat: 20.9g, Carbs: 21.2g,

    Protein: 25g, Sodium: 664mg

12. Daymio Zucchini

- Description:

  Zucchini contains vitamin A, magnesium, folate, potassium, copper, and phosphorus. This summer squash also has a high content of omega-3 fatty acids, zinc, niacin, and protein. Moreover, vitamin B1, vitamin B6, vitamin B2, and calcium in zucchini assure optimal teeth health.

- Ingredients:
  - 2 tablespoons olive oil
  - 2 zucchini, grated
  - 2 cups plain yogurt
  - 2 tablespoons walnuts, chopped

- How to prepare:
  - Heat the oil in a skillet over high heat. Cook and stir the grated zucchini for 3 minutes, stirring constantly.
  - Remove from heat and let cool. Mix the zucchini with the yogurt and walnuts, and season with salt and pepper.

- Nutritional facts:

    Calories: 170kcal, Fat: 11g, Carbs: 11g, Protein: 7g, Sodium: 92mg

13. Tropical Paradise

- Description:

  Slightly tropical with a combination of sweet strawberries and luscious mango. Ideal for breakfast or afternoon snack. This smoothie offers a wide range of vitamins and nutrients!

- Ingredients:
  - 10 ounces fresh strawberries
  - 1 cup diced mango
  - 1 cup plain low-fat yogurt
  - 1/2 cup milk
  - 1/4 cup honey
  - 4 fresh strawberries

- How to prepare:
  - Put strawberries and mango in a blender; add yogurt, milk and honey. Blend on high until smooth and thick. Pour smoothie into 4 glasses and garnish each with a fresh strawberry.

- Nutritional facts:

 Calories: 171kcal, Fat: 2g, Carbs: 36g, Protein: 6g, Sodium: 59mg

14. Maple Salmon

- Description:

  Salmon also provides important amounts of the antioxidant amino acid taurine. Salmon is an excellent source of vitamin B12, vitamin D and selenium.

- Ingredients:
  - 1/4 cup maple syrup
  - 1 tablespoon olive oil
  - 1 clove garlic, minced
  - 1/4 teaspoon garlic salt
  - 1/8 teaspoon ground black pepper
  - 1 pound salmon

- How to prepare:
  - In a small bowl, mix the maple syrup, garlic, garlic salt, and pepper.
  - Place salmon in a shallow glass baking dish, and coat with the maple syrup mixture. Cover the dish, and marinate salmon in the refrigerator 30 minutes, turning once.
  - Preheat oven to 400 degrees.

> Place the baking dish in the preheated oven, and bake salmon uncovered 20 minutes, or until easily flaked with a fork.
- Nutritional facts:

Calories: 265kcal, Fat: 12g, Carbs: 14g, Protein: 23g, Sodium: 633mg

15. Mighty Lettuce

- Description:

  Lettuce contains moisture, energy, protein, fat, carbohydrates, dietary fiber, and sugars. The minerals and vitamins found in lettuce include calcium, iron and magnesium. These three vitamins guarantee a while sparkling smile.

- Ingredients:
  - 1 head green leaf lettuce - rinsed, dried, and chopped
  - 1 red onion, sliced into rings
  - 1 pint strawberries, halved
  - 1/4 cup milk 2 tablespoons white vinegar
  - 1 tablespoon poppy seeds
  - 1/2 cup creamy salad dressing

- How to prepare:
  - Place lettuce, red onion, and strawberries in a large bowl. Place milk, vinegar, and poppy seeds in a jar with a tight-fitting lid; cover jar and shake until smooth.
  - Pour dressing over salad; toss to combine.

- Nutritional facts:

  Calories: 138kcal, Fat: 6g, Carbs: 26g, Protein: 1.8g, Sodium: 186mg

16. Corn Challenge

- Description:

  Magnesium is the most important major mineral that is needed by your body. In order to function correctly and efficiently, your body needs many nutrients. However, if it is deficient in magnesium, there are over 350 biochemical reactions that either will not occur at all or will occur very inefficiently.

- Ingredients:
  - 5 cloves garlic, minced, or more to taste
  - 2 tablespoon olive oil
  - 1 teaspoon salt
  - 1 teaspoon ground cumin
  - 1 teaspoon ground black pepper
  - 1/2 lime, juiced
  - 2 tablespoons hot pepper sauce
  - 6 ears fresh corn

- How to prepare:
  - Preheat an outdoor grill for medium heat, and lightly oil the grate.

- ➢ Heat the garlic in a small saucepan over low heat for 5 minutes. Stir together the salt, black pepper, and cumin in a small dish. Stir into the mixture along with the lime juice and hot sauce until evenly blended.
- ➢ Cook the corn on the preheated grill, rotating occasionally until the corn is hot and tender, 10 to 15 minutes.
- Nutritional facts:

Calories: 138kcal, Fat: 6g, Carbs: 26g, Protein: 1.8g, Sodium: 186mg

17. Field Marshal Broccoli

- Description:

  Broccoli is excellent for preventing cavities as it is contains calcium and fibre. These two elements reduce the chance of tooth decay and also improve the gums.

- Ingredients:
  - 2 cups broccoli florets
  - 1 yellow bell pepper, sliced
  - 1 teaspoon garlic powder
  - salt and pepper to taste
  - 1 tablespoon extra-virgin olive oil

- How to prepare:
  - Preheat an oven to 400 degrees F (200 degrees C).
  - Combine the broccoli and bell pepper in a bowl. Sprinkle garlic powder, salt and pepper over the vegetables; drizzle with the olive oil and toss to coat. Spread the vegetables into a shallow baking dish.

➤ Bake in the preheated oven until the vegetables are tender and beginning to brown, 15 to 20 minutes

- Nutritional facts:

Calories: 69kcal, Fat: 3.9g, Carbs: 8g, Protein: 2.1g, Sodium: 815mg

18. Butternut Squad

- Description:

    One cup of butternut squash provides a whopping 437% percent of your vitamin A needs for the day, as well as 52% of vitamin C and 10% or more of vitamin E, thiamin, niacin, vitamin B-6, folate, pantothenic acid and magnesium.

- Ingredients:
    - 1 butternut squash - peeled, seeded, and cut into 1-inch cubes
    - 2 tablespoons olive oil
    - 2 cloves garlic, minced

- How to prepare:
    - Preheat oven to 400 degrees F
    - Toss butternut squash with olive oil and garlic in a large bowl. Season with salt and black pepper. Arrange coated squash on a baking sheet.
    - Roast in the preheated oven until squash is tender and lightly browned, 25 to 30 minutes.

- Nutritional facts:

    Calories: 177 kcal, Fat: 7g, Carbs: 30.3g, Protein: 2.6g, Sodium: 11mg

19. Say Cheese

- Description:

  Consumption of cheese increases dental plaque pH and prevents tooth erosion. Higher the pH levels, lower the chance of developing cavities.

- Ingredients:
  - 2 cups spinach leaves
  - 1/2 apple - peeled, cored, and diced
  - 2 ounces crumbled goat cheese
  - 2 ounces walnuts

- How to prepare:
  - Put 1 cup spinach into each of 2 bowls.
  - Sprinkle apple, goat cheese, and walnuts over the spinach.

- Nutritional facts:

  Calories: 313 kcal, Fat: 2g, Carbs: 10g, Protein: 11g, Sodium: 171mg

20. Three Cheese Meeting

- Description:

  Cheese helps reduce cavities forming in teeth because it neutralises plaque acid. The higher the pH level (the more alkaline) on the surface of teeth, the more teeth are protected against dental erosion, which causes cavities and leads to fillings.

- Ingredients:
  - 1 large head leaf lettuce - rinsed, dried and torn into bite-size pieces
  - 1 cup cubed Swiss cheese
  - 1 cup crumbled feta cheese
  - 1 cup shredded Parmesan cheese
  - 1 cup toasted pecan pieces
  - 1/2 cup olive oil
  - 1/2 cup white balsamic vinegar
  - 1 tablespoon freshly ground black pepper

- How to prepare:
  - Combine lettuce, Swiss cheese, feta cheese, Parmesan cheese and pecans in a large bowl.

In a small bowl, whisk together oil, vinegar and pepper. Add dressing to salad and toss well.

- Nutritional facts:

  Calories: 618 kcal, Fat: 53.9g, Carbs: 13g, Protein: 74g, Sodium: 639mg

21. Broccoli Shield

- Description:

  Broccoli is an excellent source of vitamin B1, magnesium, omega-3 fatty acids, protein, zinc, calcium, iron, niacin and selenium.

- Ingredients:
  - 1 head fresh broccoli, cut into florets
  - 1 tablespoon olive oil
  - 2 tablespoons lemon juice
  - 1/4 cup blanched slivered almonds

- How to prepare:
  - Steam or boil broccoli until tender, approximately 4 to 8 minutes. Drain.
  - In a small saucepan, melt olive oil over medium low heat. Remove from heat.
  - Stir in lemon juice and almonds. Pour over hot broccoli, and serve.

- Nutritional facts:

  Calories: 170 kcal, Fat: 15.2g, Carbs: 7g, Protein: 3.7g, Sodium: 107mg, Cholesterol: 31mg

22. Olympic Peanuts

- Description:

  Magnesium is found in peanuts, which are essential to strengthen the bones. But peanuts also contain calcium and iron, which are important for strong teeth and bones.

- Ingredients:
  - 1 pound raw peanuts, in shells
- How to prepare:
  - Preheat oven to 500 degrees F (260 degrees C).
  - Arrange peanuts in a single layer on a cookie sheet, and place in the preheated oven.
  - Turn oven off. Leave peanuts in oven for 1 hour without opening door. Serve warm or at room temperature.
- Nutritional facts:

  Calories: 322kcal, Fat: 27.9g, Carbs: 9.2g, Protein: 14.6g, Sodium: 10mg

23. Dates on a Date

- Description:

  Magnesium, calcium, iron, vitamin B and iron are vital for dental hygiene and maintaining healthy teeth and gums. And dates are the best source for these components. Kale and Almost add a big boost to your immunity system.

- Ingredients:
  - 1 bunch kale, stems removed and discarded
  - 1 pound dates
  - 1 cup whole roasted unsalted almonds

- How to prepare:
  - Tear each kale leaf into two halves.
  - Split the dates in half, removing the pit. Place an almond in each date half in the space left by the pit.
  - Wrap each date half in a kale leaf half; pierce each with a toothpick to keep wrapped.

- Nutritional facts:

  Calories: 291kcal, Fat: 9.6g, Carbs: 51.7g, Protein: 7g, Sodium: 25mg

24. Raisins Undercover

- Description:

  Antioxidants like polyphenols and flavonoids present in raisins help fight bacteria. Hence raisins are considered an ingredient to prevent tooth decay.

- Ingredients:
  - 1 cup raisins
  - 1 pound carrots, shredded
  - 1/4 cup crushed pineapple in juice
  - 3 tablespoons shredded coconut
  - 1/4 teaspoon salt
  - 6 ounces low-fat yogurt

- How to prepare:
  - Soak raisins in a bowl of water until softened, about 20 minutes. Drain.
  - Combine carrots, raisins, pineapple, coconut, and salt in a bowl. Add yogurt and stir into carrot mixture. Cover and refrigerate until chilled.

- Nutritional facts:

    Calories: 170kcal, Fat: 6.6g, Carbs: 28g, Protein: 2g, Sodium: 125mg

25. Veteran Fig

- Description:

  Figs are essential for preventing cavities as they increase the minerals that defend the teeth. Figs are also rich in fiber which is essential for increasing saliva in the mouth.

- Ingredients:
  - 4 cups arugula
  - 8 fresh figs, quartered
  - 1/4 cup grated Parmesan cheese
  - 2 tablespoons toasted pine nuts
  - 2 tablespoons honey
  - 2 tablespoons balsamic vinegar

- How to prepare:
  - Toss arugula, figs, Parmesan cheese, and pine nuts together in a large bowl.
  - Drizzle honey and balsamic vinegar over salad before serving.

- Nutritional facts:

  Calories: 160kcal, Fat: 4.1g, Carbs: 28g, Protein: 4.2g, Sodium: 85mg

26. Boosted Green Tea

- Description:

  Green tea or tea without sugar or cream, that is, black tea is excellent for fighting bacteria. Prevent cavities by sipping on green tea. It also inhibits the growth of plaque.

- Ingredients:
  - 1 piece lemon zest
  - 2 teaspoons boiling water
  - 2 teaspoons green tea powder
  - 3/4 cup hot water
  - 1/2 cup freshly squeezed grapefruit juice
  - 3 tablespoons freshly squeezed lemon juice
  - 1 teaspoon honey

- How to prepare:
  - Put lemon zest into a large cup or mug. Cover with 2 teaspoons boiling water and let steep for about 3 minutes. Stir in the green tea powder and hot water. Add the grapefruit juice, lemon juice and honey. Mix well and serve.

- Nutritional facts:

    Calories: 89kcal, Fat: 0.1g, Carbs: 22.5g, Protein: 1.2g, Sodium: 9mg

27. Brazilian Cavity Fighters

- Description:

  Brazil nuts contain calcium, but are also rich in magnesium and iron, which are fundamental in strengthening the teeth and preventing gum-related problems.

- Ingredients:
  - 2 tablespoons sesame seeds
  - 55g (1/3 cup) sunflower seed kernels
  - 60g (1/3 cup) pepitas (pumpkin seed kernels)
  - 160g (1 cup) Brazil nuts
  - 2 tablespoons honey
  - 1 1/2 teaspoons ground cumin
  - Large pinch of ground chilli

- How to prepare:
  - Combine the seeds and almonds in a frying pan and stir over medium heat for 3-4 minutes or until lightly toasted.
  - Add honey, cumin and chilli and cook, tossing, for 1 minute. Set aside to cool.

- Nutritional facts:

    Calories: 327 kcal, Fat: 26g, Carbs: 11g, Protein: 11g, Sodium: 6.22mg

28. Almond Dream

- Description:

    Almonds or almond milk are instrumental in maintaining and improving gums and preventing cavities. Almonds contain calcium, which is necessary for evading dental problems.

- Ingredients:
    - 1 cup frozen blueberries
    - 1 banana
    - 1/2 cup almond milk
    - 1 tablespoon almond butter
    - water as needed

- How to prepare:
    - Combine blueberries, banana, almond milk, and almond butter in a blender; blend until smooth, adding water for a thinner smoothie.

- Nutritional facts:

    Calories: 231kcal, Fat: 11g, Carbs: 55g, Protein: 5.3g, Sodium: 162mg

29. Super Green Peas

- Description:

  The minerals present in green peas inhibit the growth of harmful bacteria and erases acid on the teeth. Besides, green peas are great for the skin, regulating blood sugar, promoting heart health, and preventing stomach cancer.

- Ingredients:
  - 1 (15 ounce) peas, drained
  - 4 ounces Cheddar cheese, cubed
  - 2 tablespoons finely chopped sweet onion
  - 1/4 cup creamy salad dressing

- How to prepare:
  -
  - In a medium serving bowl, mix together the peas, Cheddar cheese and onion. Stir in the sugar and creamy salad dressing. Chill for at least 1 hour before serving.

- Nutritional facts:

  Calories: 221kcal, Fat: 13g, Carbs: 17g, Protein: 10g, Sodium: 500mg

30. Mr Bean

- Description:

  Beans contain protein that is essential for building cells. Teeth also need protein for healthy gums and teeth.

- Ingredients:
  - 1 1/2 pounds green beans, trimmed and cut into 2 inch pieces
  - 1 1/2 cups water
  - 1 tablespoon olive oil
  - 3/4 teaspoon garlic salt
  - 1/4 teaspoon pepper
  - 1 1/2 teaspoons chopped fresh basil
  - 2 cups cherry tomato halves

- How to prepare:
  - Place beans and water in a large saucepan. Cover, and bring to a boil. Set heat to low, and simmer until tender, about 10 minutes. Drain off water, and set aside.
  - Stir in garlic, salt, pepper and basil.

➢ Add tomatoes, and cook stirring gently just until soft. Pour the tomato mixture over the green beans, and toss gently to blend.
- Nutritional facts:

   Calories: 122kcal, Fat: 8g, Carbs: 12.6g, Protein: 2.6g, Sodium: 294mg

31. Yogurt & Fruitty Guests

- Description:

  Yoghurt ensures strong teeth and healthy gums. It helps prevent cavities, build up of plaque and bad breath. But, remember to consume yoghurt without sugar and artificial flavouring.

- Ingredients:
  - 1 1/2 cups seedless grapes, halved
  - 2 stalks celery, chopped
  - 1 red apple, cored and chopped
  - 1 orange, peeled and sliced
  - 1/2 cup blackberries
  - 1/2 cup chopped walnuts
  - 1 (8 ounce) yogurt

- How to prepare:
  - Mix grapes, celery, apple, orange slices, blackberries, and walnuts in a large bowl; add yogurt and stir to coat.
  - Cover the bowl with plastic wrap and refrigerate until the salad is chilled, at least 30 minutes.

- Nutritional facts:

    Calories: 188kcal, Fat: 9g, Carbs: 26g, Protein: 5g, Sodium: 44mg

32. Bran Breakfast

- Description:

  Bran is not wholegrains but it is the outer shell of cereals like rice, corn, wheat, barley and oats. But studies suggest bran should be consumed with vitamin D to reduce the risk of tooth decay.

- Ingredients:
  - 1 cup water
  - 1/4 teaspoon ground cinnamon
  - 5 dried pitted prunes, chopped
  - 1/4 cup oat bran

- How to prepare:
  - Combine water, cinnamon and prunes in a saucepan over medium heat. Bring to a boil; stir in the oat bran and boil for 2 minutes.

- Nutritional facts:

  Calories: 161kcal, Fat: 2g, Carbs: 43g, Protein: 5g, Sodium: 10mg

33. Loyal Brown Rice

- Description:

    Brown rice is rich in magnesium and it also contains different types of B vitamins, which are essential for strengthening teeth and keeping the gums healthy.

- Ingredients:
    - 2 cups water
    - 1 cup brown rice
    - 1/4 cup diced red onion
    - 1/2 cup diced celery
    - 1/4 cup dried cranberries
    - 1/2 cup balsamic vinaigrette salad dressing
    - 1 tablespoon sugar

- How to prepare:
    - In a saucepan, bring water to a boil. Stir in rice, cover, and reduce heat to low. Simmer for 45 to 60 minutes, or until done.
    - Transfer rice to a serving bowl, and stir in onion, celery, cranberries, salad dressing and sugar. Cover, refrigerate, and serve cold.

- Nutritional facts:

    Calories: 302kcal, Fat: 10g, Carbs: 50g, Protein: 4g, Sodium: 365mg

34. Apple's Kingdom

- Description:

    Apples prevent the formation of cavities as the acid, sugar and fibre helps increase the production of saliva. Since the flow of saliva increases, bacteria levels go down.

- Ingredients:
    - 3 tablespoons raisins
    - 2 tart apples, peeled and shredded
    - 1 cup shredded pumpkin
    - 2 teaspoons lemon juice salt and pepper to taste

- How to prepare:
    - Place the raisins in a small dish and cover with hot water. Allow to stand for 30 minutes.
    - Once the raisins are plump, drain and place into a mixing bowl with the apple and pumpkin.

> Pour in the lemon juice and toss to coat. Season to taste with salt and pepper, and serve immediately.

- Nutritional facts:

Calories: 129kcal, Fat: 0.3g, Carbs: 34g, Protein: 1.2g, Sodium: 197mg

35. Milkbanana Shake

- Description:

    Bananas contain calcium which is important for strong bones. Bananas are rich in vitamin B and C and are perfect for fighting bacteria.

- Ingredients:
    - 1 banana, partially thawed and mashed
    - 1/2 cup milk, or more to taste
- How to prepare:
    - Mix banana and milk together in a cup or bowl until desired consistency is reached.
- Nutritional facts:

    Calories: 166kcal, Fat: 2.8g, Carbs: 34g, Protein: 5.3g, Sodium: 51mg

36. Bunny's Carrot

- Description:

    Carrots are a good source of antioxidant agents. Furthermore, carrots are rich in vitamin A, Vitamin C, Vitamin K, vitamin B8, pantothenic acid, folate, potassium, iron, copper, and manganese

- Ingredients:
    - 3 cups julienned carrots
    - 1 (20 ounce) pineapple rolls
    - 1 cup miniature marshmallows
    - 1/2 cup raisins
    - 1/2 cup diced celery
    - 2/3 cup creamy salad dressing
    - 1 teaspoon white sugar

- How to prepare:
    - In a large bowl, toss together the carrots, pineapple, marshmallows, raisins and celery.
    - Whisk together the salad dressing and sugar; pour over salad and toss. Chill for at least 12 hours.

- Nutritional facts:

    Calories: 198kcal, Fat: 6.4g, Carbs: 36g, Protein: 8g, Sodium: 241mg

37. Cavities Buster

- Description:

  Avocados are very nutritious and contain a wide variety of nutrients, including 20 different vitamins and minerals, ensuring that cavities will be kept away from your teeth

- Ingredients:
  - 1 avocado
  - 1/2 teaspoon garlic, minced
  - 1/2 teaspoon minced fresh ginger root
  - 1 tablespoon olive oil

- How to prepare:
  - Stir together garlic, ginger, and olive oil; set aside for five minutes to allow the flavors to blend.
  - Cut the avocado in half, and discard the pit; divide the sauce between the avocado halves.

- Nutritional facts:

  Calories: 164kcal, Fat: 15g, Carbs: 9.1g, Protein: 2.2g, Sodium: 157mg

38. Cauliflower Cinema

- Description:

  Roasting cauliflower transforms it into a delectable snack. You will eat it up just like it's popcorn. Very easy to prepare and delicious!

- Ingredients:
  - 1 tablespoon olive oil
  - 1/2 teaspoon garlic salt
  - 1 large head cauliflower, broken into small florets

- How to prepare:
  - Preheat oven to 400 degrees F (200 degrees C).
  - Whisk olive oil and garlic salt together in a large bowl; add cauliflower and toss to coat completely. Spread cauliflower out onto a baking sheet.
  - Bake in the preheated oven until golden and tender, 15 to 18 minutes.

- Nutritional facts:

  Calories: 83kcal, Fat: 3.6g, Carbs: 11.2g, Protein: 4.2g, Sodium: 290mg

39. Spotted Walnuts

- Description:

    Walnuts are high in monounsaturated and polyunsaturated fats and a good source of protein. Nuts have a reputation for being a high-calorie and high-fat food. However, they are dense in nutrients and provide heart-healthy fats

- Ingredients:
    - 2 cups walnuts
    - 2 cloves garlic, minced
    - 1 tablespoon honey
    - 1 tablespoon extra-virgin olive oil
    - 1 tablespoon minced fresh rosemary

- How to prepare:
    - Preheat oven to 350 degrees F
    - Mix walnuts, garlic, honey, olive oil, rosemary, and salt together in a bowl until walnuts are coated; spread onto the prepared baking sheet.
    - Bake in the preheated oven until walnuts are lightly browned, about 10 minutes.

- Nutritional facts:

    Calories: 183kcal, Fat: 5.8g, Carbs: 40g, Protein: 5.2g, Sodium: 42mg

40. Nectarine's Gift

- Description:

  Nectarines have a wonderful antioxidant power with a good amount of polyphenols, vitamin C content and carotenoids such as beta-carotene and cryptoxanthin. Enjoy this smoothie at any time of the day!

- Ingredients:
  - 2 large nectarines, pitted and quartered
  - 1 banana, cut into pieces and frozen
  - 1 large orange, peeled and quartered
  - 1 cup vanilla yogurt
  - 1 cup orange juice
  - 1 tablespoon honey

- How to prepare:
  - Place the nectarines, frozen banana chunks, orange, vanilla yogurt, orange juice, and honey into a blender, and blend until smooth.

- Nutritional facts:

    Calories: 163kcal, Fat: 2.8g, Carbs: 22g, Protein: 3.2g, Sodium: 12mg

41. Homemade Almond Milk

- Description:

    You can consume this milk to strengthen the teeth and prevent tooth decay. But milk should be consumed without sugar and artificial ingredients in order to prevent cavities.

- Ingredients:
    - 1 cup raw almonds
    - 3 cups water
    - 1 tablespoon honey or more to taste
    - 1 pinch sea salt

- How to prepare:
    - Place almonds in a bowl and pour in enough water to cover; soak at least 12 hours. Drain water.
    - Blend almonds and 3 cups water in a blender on low speed for 10 seconds. Turn blender off for 5 seconds. Blend almonds and water on high speed for 60 seconds. Pour mixture through cheesecloth or a nut bag into a bowl. Discard the pulp or save for another use.

- ➤ Clean the blender and return milk to blender; add agave nectar and salt. Blend milk until smooth.
- Nutritional facts:

  Calories: 440kcal, Fat: 36g, Carbs: 22g, Protein: 15g, Sodium: 177mg

42. Primal Kale Salad

- Description:

  Kale is filled with so many nutrients, vitamins, folate and magnesium. Overall, a great benefit for your teeth and gums

- Ingredients:
  - 1 bunch kale, large stems discarded, leaves finely chopped
  - 1/2 teaspoon salt
  - 1 tablespoon apple cider vinegar
  - 1 apple, diced
  - 1/3 cup feta cheese
  - 1/4 cup currants
  - 1/4 cup toasted pine nuts

- How to prepare:
  - Massage kale with salt in a large mixing bowl for 2 minutes. Pour vinegar over the kale and toss to coat. Fold apple, feta cheese, currants, and pine nuts into the kale.

- Nutritional facts:

    Calories: 102kcal, Fat: 4.8g, Carbs: 12g, Protein: 4.6g, Sodium: 277mg

43. Happy Orange Zinger

- Description:

    Oranges contain vitamin C, which is essential for fighting bacteria. Besides, oranges also help to boost immunity. This is the perfect drink for when you're feeling a little under the weather.

- Ingredients:
    - 1/2 inch piece fresh ginger root
    - 1 pound carrots, scrubbed and trimmed
    - 2 oranges, peeled

- How to prepare:
    - Juice ginger, carrots, and oranges in a juicer. Serve immediately.

- Nutritional facts:

    Calories: 188kcal, Fat: 1g, Carbs: 44g, Protein: 4.6g, Sodium: 314mg

44. Kohlrabi Celeb

- Description:

  This vegetable is full of nutrients and minerals like copper, potassium, manganese, iron, and calcium, as well as vitamins, such as vitamin C, B-complex vitamins, vitamin A, and vitamin K.

- Ingredients:
  - 1/2 onion, diced
  - 1 kohlrabi, thinly sliced
  - 1/2 pound yellow crookneck squash, sliced
  - 3 cloves garlic, crushed
  - 1/2 teaspoon salt
  - 1 teaspoon ground black pepper

- How to prepare:
  - Add onion and kohlrabi to skillet; cook and stir 5 minutes. Add yellow squash, garlic, salt, and black pepper. Cook until squash has released some liquid but is not soggy, about 10 minutes. Serve immediately.

- Nutritional facts:

    Calories: 53kcal, Fat: 2g, Carbs: 4g, Protein: 2g, Sodium: 120mg

45. Rolled Prawns

- Description:

  Shrimp are a low-fat source of protein. A 3-ounce serving of shrimp, roughly 15 to 16 large shrimp, or approximately 8 prawns, contains 101 calories per serving, over 19 grams of protein and only 1.4 grams of total fat. A serving also contains calcium, potassium and phosphorus and is a good source of vitamins A and E.

- Ingredients:
  - 1/2 cup olive oil
  - 1 tablespoon mustard
  - 3 cloves garlic, minced
  - 1 lemon, juiced
  - 1 orange, juiced
  - 1 teaspoon dried basil
  - 30 tiger prawns, peeled and deveined

- How to prepare:
  - In a glass dish, mix together the olive oil, mustard, garlic, lemon juice and orange juice.

Add the prawns, and stir to coat. Cover, and let marinate for 1 hour.

- ➢ Heat an outdoor grill to high heat.
- ➢ Thread prawns onto skewers. Grill for 3 to 5 minutes, turning once, until pink.

- Nutritional facts:

Calories: kcal, Fat: g, Carbs: g, Protein: g, Sodium: mg

46. Classic Fruits

- Description:

  Packed with vitamins, an excellent smoothie that keeps cavities away and strenghtens your gums.

- Ingredients:
  - 4 ice cubes
  - 1/4 fresh pineapple - peeled, cored and cubed
  - 1 large banana, cut into chunks
  - 1 cup pineapple or apple juice
- How to prepare:
  - Place ice cubes, pineapple, banana, and pineapple juice into the bowl of a blender. Puree on high until smooth.

  Nutritional facts:

  Calories: 313kcal, Fat: 0.9g, Carbs: 78.7g, Protein: 3g, Sodium: 10mg

ADDITIONAL TITLES FROM THIS AUTHOR

70 Effective Meal Recipes to Prevent and Solve Being Overweight: Burn Fat Fast by Using Proper Dieting and Smart Nutrition

By

Joe Correa CSN

48 Acne Solving Meal Recipes: The Fast and Natural Path to Fixing Your Acne Problems in Less Than 10 Days!

By

Joe Correa CSN

41 Alzheimer's Preventing Meal Recipes: Reduce or Eliminate Your Alzheimer's Condition in 30 Days or Less!

By

Joe Correa CSN

70 Effective Breast Cancer Meal Recipes: Prevent and Fight Breast Cancer with Smart Nutrition and Powerful Foods

By

Joe Correa CSN

www.ingramcontent.com/pod-product-compliance
Lightning Source LLC
Chambersburg PA
CBHW052121070526
44586CB00016B/2030